# THE
# GOOD NEWS
## OF
# EASTER

ROUSSEAUX BRASSEUR | ART BY SIAN JAMES

HARVEST HOUSE PUBLISHERS
EUGENE, OREGON

**Rousseaux Brasseur** is a storyteller born, raised, and still residing in Southern Oregon. He's an old soul filled with childlike faith whose life mission is to lead children into the love of the Father, the truth of Jesus, and the joy of the Holy Spirit. He is the author of *The Good News of Christmas* and *The Pilgrim's Progress: A Poetic Retelling of John Bunyan's Classic Tale*. Rousseaux and his beloved, Hannah Georgia Rose Petal, dwell by a creek in the most peaceful of all places.
Find Rousseaux at www.QuesterCommunity.com and on YouTube as The Quester.

**Sian James'** vibrant and imaginative illustrations have appeared in projects for several prominent clients, including HarperCollins and Penguin Random House. She currently resides in Cambridge, England, with her husband, her daughter, and their affectionate cats, Miso and Mochi. Connect with her and learn more at www.sianjamesillustration.com and on Instagram @sianjart.

The Scripture quotation of John 11:25-26 is taken from the Holy Bible, New International Version®, NIV®. Copyright © 1973, 1978, 1984, 2011 by Biblica, Inc.™ Used with permission of Zondervan. All rights reserved worldwide. www.zondervan.com. The "NIV" and "New International Version" are trademarks registered in the United States Patent and Trademark Office by Biblica, Inc.™

Cover design by Faceout Studio, Tim Green. Interior design by Left Coast Design.

For bulk, special sales, or ministry purchases, please call 1-800-547-8979.
Email: CustomerService@hhpbooks.com

This logo is a federally registered trademark of the Hawkins Children's LLC. Harvest House Publishers, Inc., is the exclusive licensee of this trademark.

## THE GOOD NEWS OF EASTER

Copyright © 2025 by Rousseaux Brasseur
Artwork copyright © 2025 by Sian James
Published by Harvest House Publishers
Eugene, Oregon 97408
www.harvesthousepublishers.com

ISBN 978-0-7369-8923-7 (hardcover)

Library of Congress Control Number: 2024942256

Printed in China

24 25 26 27 28 29 30 31 32 / RDS / 10 9 8 7 6 5 4 3 2 1

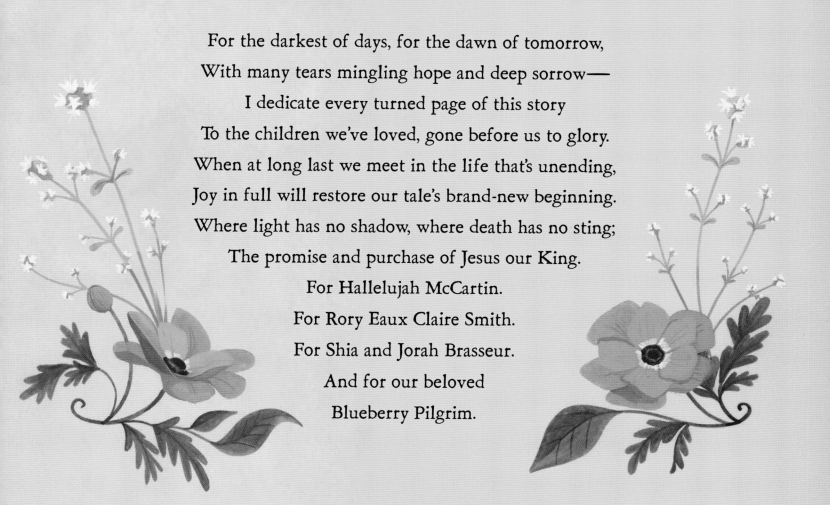

For the darkest of days, for the dawn of tomorrow,

With many tears mingling hope and deep sorrow—

I dedicate every turned page of this story

To the children we've loved, gone before us to glory.

When at long last we meet in the life that's unending,

Joy in full will restore our tale's brand-new beginning.

Where light has no shadow, where death has no sting;

The promise and purchase of Jesus our King.

For Hallelujah McCartin.

For Rory Eaux Claire Smith.

For Shia and Jorah Brasseur.

And for our beloved

Blueberry Pilgrim.

I wish to remind my readers now before this tale goes on,
That the shade and shadows of night must pass before the
light of dawn.
Although at midnight darkness hides the sun's
abundant rays,
The morning always comes again and sets the sky ablaze!

Now open your eyes, your heart, and your mind to the world's most wonderful story...

Of the Light from above, the Son of God's Love—the King of grace and glory!

The news had spread of the miracle worker, Jesus the Nazarene,
Acclaimed as Israel's promised Messiah and long-awaited King!

But this King wore no glittering armor for an army to adore.

He sat not on a stallion bred for battle or for war.

He wore no sword. He wore no crown. He wore no royal robe.
Through Jerusalem on a donkey's colt, their humble King now rode.

Upon the road folks laid their cloaks with branches cut from palms,
They hailed their Lord with chants and roared out praises from the Psalms:
"Blessed be our saving King who in God's name has come!
Hosanna in the Highest! Glory be to David's Son!"

But jealous Jewish leaders scoffed and plotted an awful scheme—
To arrest and put to death this man, rejecting Him as King.

But evil plots could never stop God's great plan of salvation—
To sacrifice His own life and redeem His whole creation.

That week the Passover feast was spread. Giving thanks, Jesus took
    and broke the bread.
"This is My body. Take and eat. Remember Me always," the Savior said;
Then Jesus lifted up the cup. "This is My blood, which cleanses all sin;
But till we're in My Father's kingdom I will not drink its wine again."

Shock shook them all as Jesus warned, "A traitor is at hand.
And Peter, too, before the rooster crows, will deny the Son of Man."

When the sacred meal was finished, Jesus stood and left His seat.
Then He went and found a basin and towel and knelt to wash their feet.

"I am your teacher and your Lord, so do just as I've done for you.
The greatest in My kingdom serve, as you have seen Me do."

When this was done, all but one followed Jesus to a garden to pray.
But as they slept, King Jesus wept and pleaded for another way.

"Abba, Father, if You are willing, remove this cup from My hands! Yet not My will, but Yours be done. Fulfill all of Your plans."

Then Judas, the traitor, approached with a mob. Jesus asked,
"Whom do you seek?"
His betrayer came forth with the secret sign and kissed Him on
the cheek.

"The hour of darkness's power has come," said the Son whose
hands were bound.
Then seized by dread, the disciples fled from Gethsemane's garden
ground.

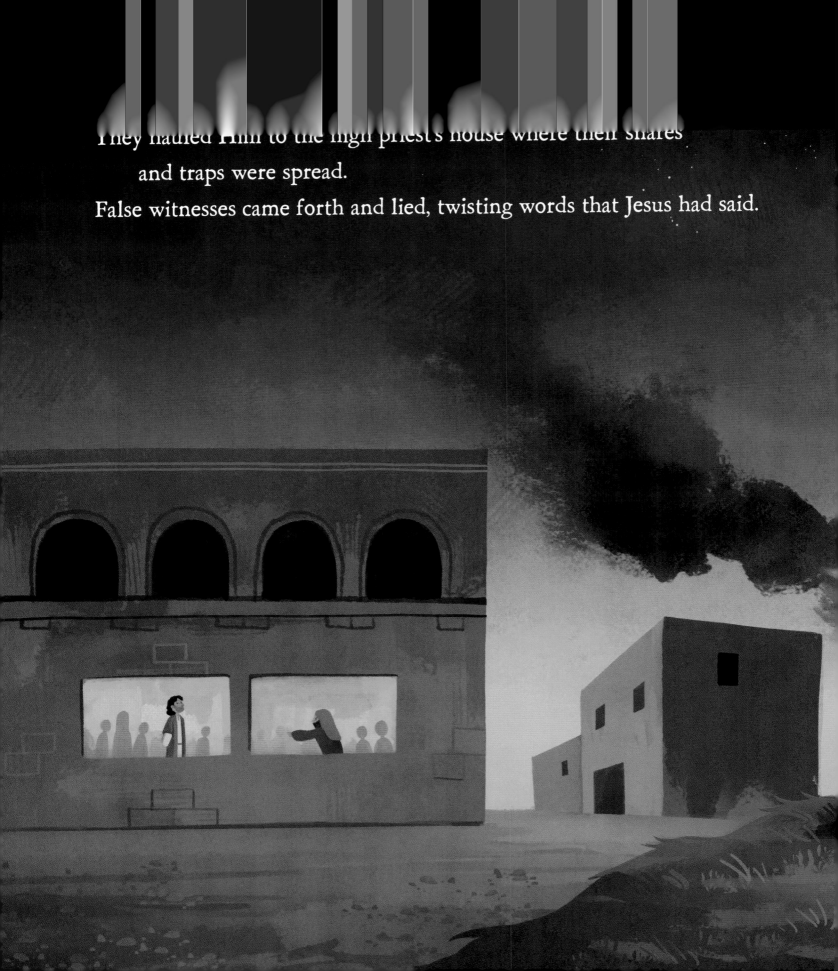

They hauled Him to the high priest's house where their snares
and traps were spread.
False witnesses came forth and lied, twisting words that Jesus had said.

Now Peter followed and stood by the fire, watching his Rabbi's trial,
But when asked if he was His disciple, he lied three times in denial.
Then the rooster crowed as Jesus had warned. Peter wept and fled in
   shame,
While Jesus, the only blameless man, stood bearing our guilt and blame.

"Are You the Christ, the Son of God? Tell us!" they shouted in demand.
"I AM. And you will see the Son of Man seated in power at God's right hand!"

"Blasphemy! Take Him to Pontius Pilate! He deserves to be crucified!"
But the Roman ruler refused to do anything till Jesus stood trial inside.

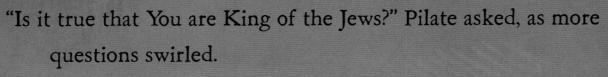

"Is it true that You are King of the Jews?" Pilate asked, as more
questions swirled.
"I've come from above as God's witness to Truth. My kingdom is not
of this world."

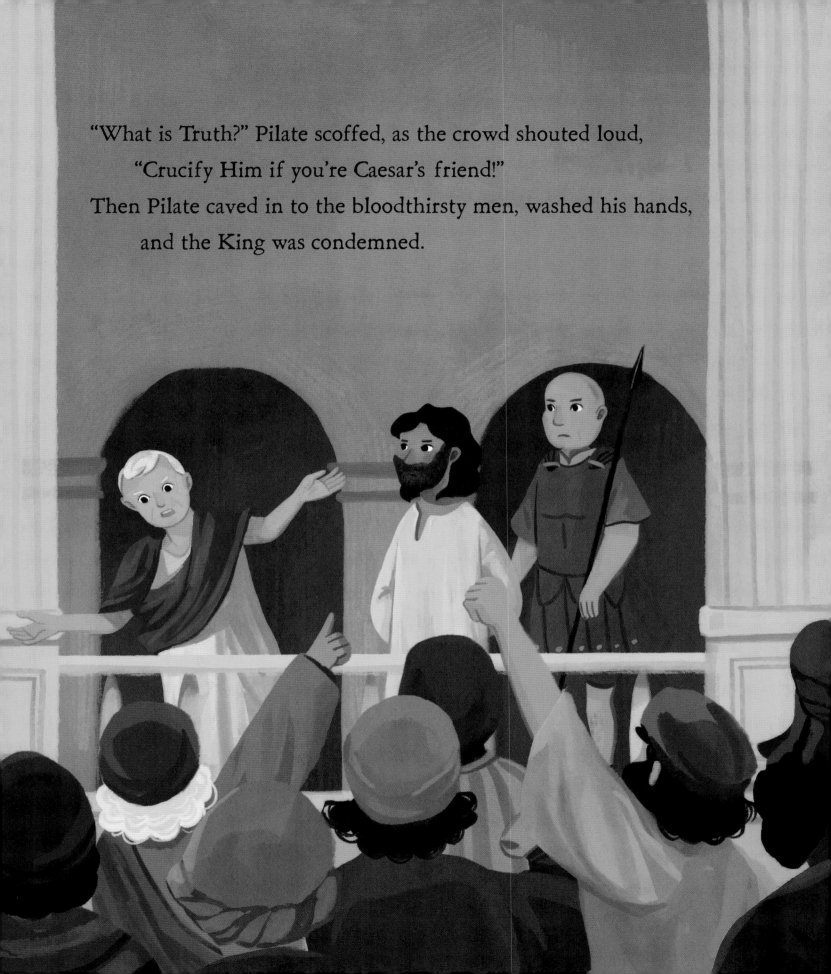

"What is Truth?" Pilate scoffed, as the crowd shouted loud,
"Crucify Him if you're Caesar's friend!"
Then Pilate caved in to the bloodthirsty men, washed his hands,
and the King was condemned.

God's spotless, sinless, silent Lamb was despised and rejected in scorn—
They robed Him and placed earth's curse on His head: a cruel,
    twisted crown of thorns.
"Hail the King of the Jews!" they mocked as they spat in His face and
    whipped His skin,
But all this pain, disgrace, and shame was God's way of claiming the
    blame for our sin.

Then high upon the skull-shaped hill, they nailed King Jesus to the cross.
And as foretold in the Psalms of old, for His clothing the soldiers cast lots.
The crowd hurled taunts, "If You're God's Son, come down, and we'll trust
in You!"
But Jesus responded, "Father, forgive them! They know not what they do."
But at that hour a darkness fell, which blackened every spark of light,
As evil's power, human hate, and God's judgment for sin came down
on Christ.

"It is finished!" He cried. Then looking up, He gasped one final breath,
"Father, into Your hands I commit My Spirit!" Then Jesus bowed in death.
Inside the temple, the curtain tore! Close by, the rocks and tombs split open!
The world was shaken to its core. The disciples' hearts were broken.

They took His body off the cross and carried it to a nearby tomb.
A stone was rolled to seal His grave—all hope was buried with
Him in gloom.

Then Pilate sent a soldier squadron to seal the stone and stand on guard,
To keep the King locked up in His tomb, which they assumed would not
be hard.

But God the Father Almighty promised to resurrect His sinless King.

The Spirit of Life would reverse sin's curse and break Death's dreadful sting!

And just before the Sunday sun awoke and rose in the crimson sky,

The Son of God and Son of Man was miraculously raised and came alive!

His heart pumped out. His lungs swelled up as He breathed the sweet air in.
He felt the chill of darkness still as He stretched His sleepy limbs!
An angel bright with heaven's light rolled the stone from His burial room!
The soldiers fled as the Lord left the dead, never again to return to a tomb.

Like a seed, three days buried in the earth, the body of Jesus was planted,

But just like the spring, He arose to bring new life for all the planet!

Set free from Death's prison, the King who had risen first greeted
 Mary Magdalene,

And for forty more days after Jesus was raised, He appeared to all
 of His friends!

To those who groaned on Emmaus Road, He was shown and made known by breaking bread.
The ten with them in Jerusalem then worshipped Him who rose from the dead!

The scar-bearing Savior eight days later saved Thomas from doubt
and disbelief.

Once more on the shore, the Lord restored Peter and freed him of
guilt and grief.

Before His ascension He met all His friends on a mountain, where
    Jesus proclaimed,
"All authority has been given to Me in heaven and on earth to reign!

Go announce this Good News to every nation! Make disciples of all
   who hear it,
Baptize them in the name of the Father, the Son, and the Holy Spirit.
Teach them to obey the commands of the King...and whether you're
   near or far,
Behold, I am with you to the end of all things, wherever in the world
   you are!"

Then lifting up His hands to bless the disciples who gathered around,
The King of glory was lifted up and ascended off the ground!

All heaven and earth erupted in worship, as the resurrected Son of Man
Reclaimed His glorious heavenly throne and sat down at His Father's

Not a thing that King Jesus had said or done was random
or happenstance—
He fulfilled the prophecies, purposes, and plan that God
promised long in advance.
The Holy Spirit inspired the truths which poured from each prophet's pen,
So that every word in the whole of Holy Scripture points perfectly
to Him!

But the whole of His story has more grace and glory than a world full of books could contain,

Yet these things are written so that you might believe and receive eternal life in His name!

Jesus said to her, "I am the
resurrection and the life. The one
who believes in me will live, even
though they die; and whoever lives
by believing in me will never die.
Do you believe this?"

JOHN 11:25-26